Halloween

with matthew mead

D0509104

Halloween
with matthew mead

ALL PHOTOGRAPHY BY MATTHEW MEAD UNLESS OTHERWISE NOTED.

OXMOOR HOUSE

VP, Publishing Director Jim Childs

Editorial Director Leah McLaughlin

Creative Director Felicity Keane

Brand Manager Nina Fleishman

Senior Editors Rebecca Brennan, Heather Averett, Andrea C. Kirkland, MS, RD

Managing Editor Rebecca Benton

THEI

Publisher Richard Fraiman

VP, Strategy and Business Development Steven Sandonato

Executive Director, Marketing Services Carol Pittard

Executive Director, Retail and Special Sales Tom Mifsud

Executive Publishing Director Joy Butts

Editorial Director Stephen Koepp

Editorial Operations Director Michael Q. Bullerdick

Director, Bookazine Development and Marketing Laura Adam

Finance Director Glenn Buonocore

Associate Publishing Director Megan Pearlman

General Counsel Helen Wan

Founder, Creative Director, Editor in Chief Matthew Mead

Managing Editor Jennifer Mead

Executive Editor Linda MacDonald

Senior Writer Sarah Egge

Contributing Lifestyle Editor Stephanie Nielson

Art Director Doug Turshen

Graphic Designer David Huang

Studio Assistants/Designers Lisa Bisson and Lisa Smith-Renauld

THANK YOU to everyone who participated in the creation of this magazine including: Abby Bisson; Robert Brawley, his wife Cheryl and their children; Michelle, Chaz, Sam & Eliana Coffin; David, Brandy, and Natalie Dubuc; Lisa Fantasia of Wicked Sweets; Billy and Tommy Fraser; J.M. and Parker Hirsch; Alison Ladman of the Crust and Crumb Bakery; the Langlais family; Michelle Leiter; Jill McCullough and Tim Meeh of Northfield Farm in Canterbury, New Hampshire; Debra Norton of Vintage Paper Parade; Andrew and Emily Pollack; Alexandria Tobey; Mary and Gordon Welch.

With any craft project, check product labels to make sure that the materials you use are safe and nontoxic. The instructions in this book are intended to be followed with adult supervision.

NOTE: Neither the publisher not the author is responsible for your specific health or allergy needs that may require medical supervision, or for any adverse reactions to the recipes contained in this book.

ISBN 10: 0-8487-3813-6
ISBN 13: 978-0-8487-3813-6

editor's letter

THE JOLLY ROGER Just as a sailing ship that suddenly hoists this pirate's flag goes from ordinary to threatening, things are not what they seem on Halloween. A holiday filled with magic and masquerade, it's the one time of year when people and objects can disguise themselves as something else. And I love every minute of it!

We've captured the fun of this subterfuge by featuring the best ways to make everyday objects more imaginative and compelling. Embellish delicious cookies to look like cleavers and poison bottles. Dress plain pumpkins in jaunty polka dots. Give your rooms a seasonal lift from black-and-white decorations. Even get-togethers for friends—children or adults—become extra-special this time of year, thanks to inventive themes.

You'll find no illusion, however, in the easy ideas and instructions that are my hallmarks. Supplies come from local stores and friendly online sites, and many times you'll be able to upcycle what you already have. Recipes are tested to come out right—and tasty—every time. Trust me, my team and I have already tried them all.

Though I love the surprising and thrilling aspects of Halloween, I want to make your celebration of it as chills-free as possible. Share your experiences and stories with me at HolidayWithMatthewMead.com. I'm always listening.

Keep up with HALLOWEEN, find all the free project templates and recipes you could want, and enjoy a preview of HOLIDAY at HolidayWithMatthewMead.com.

Look for our next issue, the HOLIDAY Christmas special, on newsstands in October.

CARD TRICKS

Pick our brains to create ghoulish handmade
greetings and spirited display ideas for
your friends and favorite trick-or-treaters.

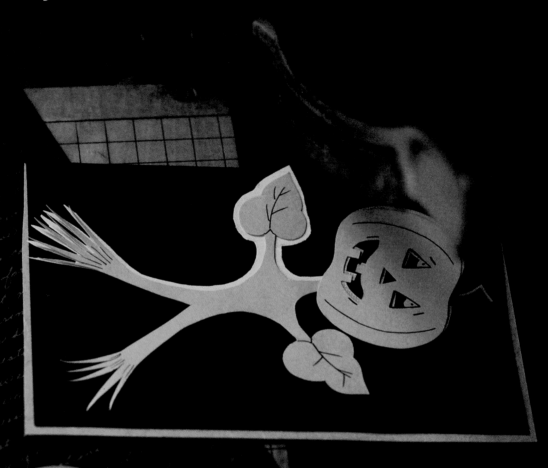

SPIRITED GREETING

Making and displaying Halloween
cards can be a fun way to share your
enthusiasm for the season and add
some engaging décor to your home.
Use vintage or store-bought cards, or
create your own greetings to highlight
the playful side of Halloween. Paper is
inexpensive and easy to use. Gather the
kids for a craft session to fold and cut
paper into cards (this page) that can
be layered with cut-outs and stickers.
Often too charming to toss after the
holiday, Halloween cards can be brought
out year after year and displayed in
imaginative ways for affordably festive
décor. Anchor branches in a vase with
black stones (opposite) and nestle your
cards in the branches.

WHAT DID
PETER PETER
USE TO COVER
HIS BLACK EYE?

a pumpkin patch

HAPPY HALLOWEEN

WHOO'S FUNNY?

Enlist the help of a Halloween joke book or perform a Google search to assist you in writing your own clever Halloween salutations. Matthew made up this joke (opposite) for his annual fall garden club lecture. He received so many laughs he likes to re-use it again and again for his own Halloween cards. To create a card like it, download the owl silhouette at HolidayWithMatthewMead.com and cut it out for your own card. Pumpkin buttons from the crafts store can be hot-glued on or stitched to the inside of the card. Consider creating two of the cards and display both in a shadow box or dual photo frame to showcase the inside and outside of the card. Arrange cards in unusual ways for decorative impact. Here, the owl card (this page) seeks shelter in a vintage wrought-iron lantern.

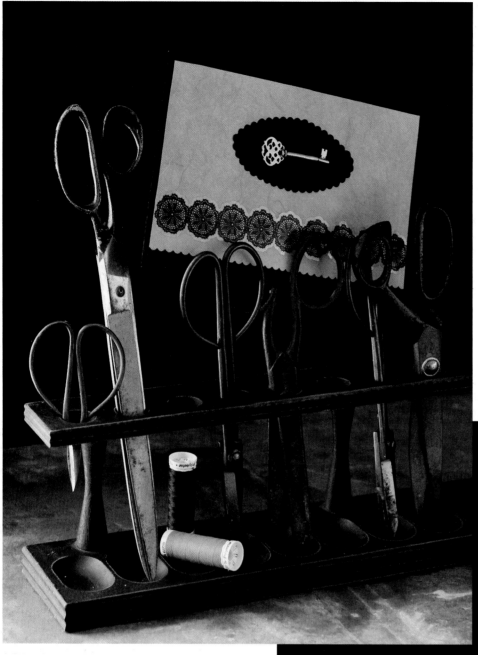

A STICKY SITUATION

Scrapbook supply stores offer a great selection of Halloween stickers, embellishments and cut-outs to adorn your ghostly welcomes. Use card stock or scrapbook paper to create spirited invitations and greeting cards for every occasion. We trimmed a folded piece of orange cardstock (this page, above) using scalloped-edged scissors and adhered it to a sheet of trimmed black scrapbook paper, adorning it with stickers for flourish. Old scissors in a vintage pipe stand offer up an unexpected display option. A simple jack o'lantern greeting card can be crafted using black construction paper and scissors. Its cheery grin adds whimsy when tucked into the spokes of a vintage rubber stamp holder (this page, right). Display favorite cards – decorated with rubber skeleton stickers from the crafts store – in the teeth of an orange-painted flower frog (opposite).

"A trip to the crafts store is all you need to create these adorable Halloween greetings. Keep it simple, but make it spooky!" *— Matthew*

SPARKLY SPOOKY

Get inspired by objects you already own that have the potential to spook. We cut out a silhouette of a candelabrum (opposite) from scrapbook paper and embellished it with stickers. Displayed alongside a small-scale candelabrum Matthew borrowed from his stash, it complements its flickering friend. A black iron plant stand atop a metal table elevates the vignette, underscoring its regal air. To create a similar card, look for candelabra or chandelier stickers in the scrapbooking aisle of most craft supply stores. A simple black cardstock greeting (this page) is made sparkly with an assortment of glittered stickers, including a glittery pumpkin with a dazzling smile. Set into the bristles of a fireplace broom and propped near a hearth, the card is in good company with a cast of orange and black accessories, including a pumpkin-filled urn and a vintage pitcher.

THREE RING FLING

Forge a new trick-or-treating tradition with a circus-inspired barn bash that celebrates the art of clowning around.

COME ONE, COME ALL

Halloween parties have become popular with parents as a safe alternative to the door-to-door candy hunt. Take advantage of unexpected venues like a large barn (opposite) or bring in hay bales to set the scene in your garage. Overturned aluminum troughs (this page), decorated with colorful acrylic paint, fill in as vintage-inspired circus stands and help set the carnival theme.

SET THE STAGE Offer ready-made treats as favors and prizes. **1.** Circus transfers are ironed on to muslin bags (from Etsy.com/Shop/VintagePaperParade) filled with fireballs and animal figures. **2.** Embellish paper treat bags with labels made using craft store stamps, and fill with super balls, jacks, and circus-themed playing cards. **3.** Send out a box of Barnum's Animal Crackers® with ticket invitations for a fun surprise. **4.** An old box with a themed stencil and découpaged tiger sticker stands in as a spot to sit and have a snack. **OPPOSITE :** The decorated barn offers a casual, fun space where thrills abound and spills are no big deal. Extra-large beach balls offer extra seating and are fun to toss around or bounce upon.

Trained
Seal

Balloon
Man

Flying
Lady

Laughing
Lion

Lion
Tamer

Bareback
Rider

Wild
Man

Royal
Ringmaster

Strong
Man

GO VINTAGE

Look for circus-themed playing cards, vintage planters, and peanut bags on Etsy and eBay to give your party authentic carnival flair. Use the cards (opposite) for games of Memory and fill the ceramic planter (this page) with sacks of roasted and salted peanuts in the shell. Simple cut-out paper stars dress up the tiered plant stand used to display all of the party snacks.

CIRCUS TRAPPINGS

1. Create a guest book by découpaging an old book with a circus elephant print. **2.** Paper masks on sticks are fuss-free and kids can have fun trading them on a whim. **3.** Set up a photo booth area complete with a ring master costume so everyone can try out this coveted role. A thrift shop blazer and top hat is all you'll need. **4.** Create circus-animal masks by enlarging images from Dover copyright-free books. Cut out holes for the eyes and attach the masks to pieces of decorative moldings. **5.** Paper elephants on sticks are a fun way to dress up the space (find similar images in Dover books). **6.** A top hat or derby encourages everyone to clown around. **7.** A calendar of vintage circus posters becomes inspiring wall art in the barn. **8.** Use the party décor as fun props for impromptu group shots (opposite).

CLOWNING AROUND
Keep the food fun and ready-made. Ice cream cups in chocolate and strawberry (opposite) are instant treats, and are ready to eat using stamped wooden spoons (from Etsy.com/Shop/VintagePaperParade). Set vintage clown cake toppers from Etsy (this page) into fresh coconut marshmallows that were purchased from a local candy shop and placed in cheery cupcake wrappers.

1 **2**

3 **4**

CARNIVAL FARE Offer guests some healthy treats to offset their candy cravings. **1.** Poke clown toppers into watermelon slices for slurpy snacks parents will appreciate. **2.** Bake-and-serve pretzels easily go from the freezer, to the oven, to the hands of eager guests. **3.** Have extra spoons and napkins on hand to prevent sticky fingers and faces. **4.** Dress up a store-bought cake with cereal hair, black icing eyes, a licorice mouth, and a nose fashioned from a cinnamon wafer and red gum ball.
OPPOSITE: Offer lemonade and a "help yourself" buffet, and sit back to watch the kids recreate "the greatest show on earth." Hang pennant banners crafted from scrapbook paper throughout the barn for colorful décor that kids can help make.

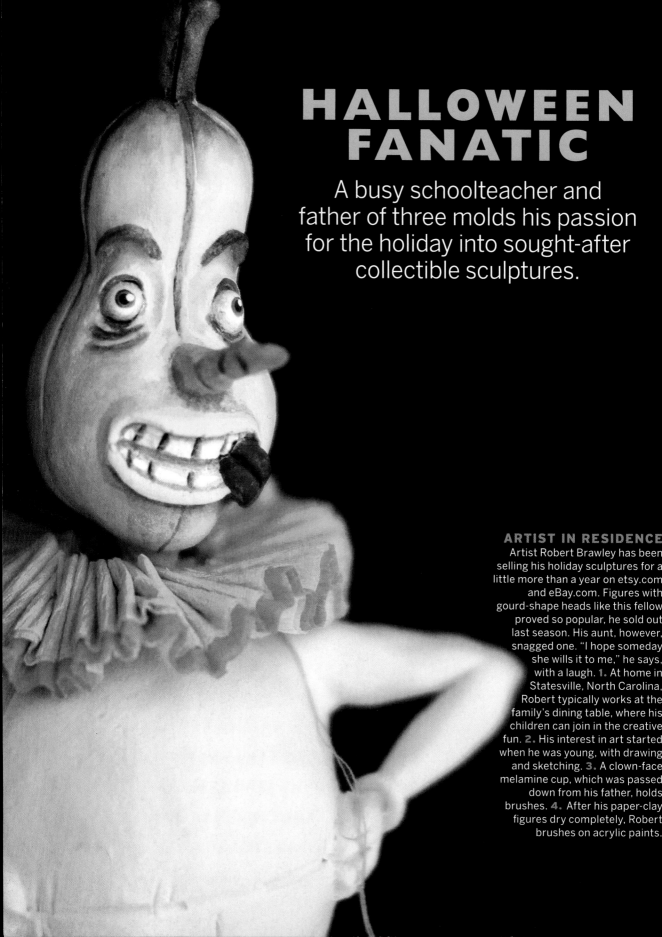

HALLOWEEN FANATIC

A busy schoolteacher and father of three molds his passion for the holiday into sought-after collectible sculptures.

ARTIST IN RESIDENCE

Artist Robert Brawley has been selling his holiday sculptures for a little more than a year on etsy.com and eBay.com. Figures with gourd-shape heads like this fellow proved so popular, he sold out last season. His aunt, however, snagged one. "I hope someday she wills it to me," he says, with a laugh. **1.** At home in Statesville, North Carolina, Robert typically works at the family's dining table, where his children can join in the creative fun. **2.** His interest in art started when he was young, with drawing and sketching. **3.** A clown-face melamine cup, which was passed down from his father, holds brushes. **4.** After his paper-clay figures dry completely, Robert brushes on acrylic paints.

1 2

3 4

CHANCES ARE if you're reading this, you are fond of Halloween. More than fond even. But fanatical about it? Artist Robert Brawley happily crosses that line—and then advertises it. His blog and his business, even the works he creates, carry the name of his alter ego, The Halloween Fanatic. "I've just always loved Halloween," he explains simply. Robert started collecting Halloween pieces in the late '90s, and eventually he gained enough tips and ideas from his friends in the online folk art community to tap into his art background and start creating his own pieces. Friendly and quick to laugh (and not in the maniacal way you'd expect of a fanatic), Robert teaches elementary school and, with his wife Cheryl, is raising twin 6-year-old girls and a 5-year-old son. How does he find time to slip into "fanatic" mode and create the expressive, imaginative figures that have quickly gained a passionate following and notice in the folk art world? After dinner. Most evenings, weekends, and summer-vacation days, he spreads out his wood dowels, acrylic paints, brushes, and mounds of paper clay on the dining table. "The girls have really gotten into art this year," he says. "It's great family time." Does Cheryl, a nurse, share his passion for Halloween? "Not really, which is funny," he says, laughing. "But she's really supportive of it. I sculpt things for other holidays, like Easter, just to give her a break. But when I am making bunnies, I can't wait to get back to Halloween. There's something about the orange and black that I really enjoy."

FRIENDLY FACES
There's a sense of humor in Robert's work, such as this vulnerable Frankenstein who wears his heart broadly (opposite), and a jack-'o-lantern who carries himself like a pompous politician. "I lean toward the whimsical and the joy it brings to kids," he says. "I wouldn't make anything I wouldn't want the kids to see."

A FAMILY AFFAIR

Robert's children have the same passion for Halloween. **1.** A springtime rabbit is clearly ready for this fall event. **2.** Lily, 6, shows off a witch with an equally gap-toothed smile. **3.** Many of Robert's sculptures can be hung as ornaments. **4.** Hannah balances a stuffed pumpkin that crosses over from Halloween to Thanksgiving decoration. **5.** Twinkle, a Boston terrier-and-pug mix, inspires many of Robert's creations, including the home page of his web site, TwinklesSalesDepartment.blogspot.com. **6.** Two black crows herald the start of the holiday. **7.** Lucas, 5, has a favorite green monster. **8.** A carved version of Twinkle plays ball. **OPPOSITE:** Holiday decorations include Robert's own pieces, as well as mercury glass pumpkins.

1

2

3

4

5

6

7

8

MASQUERADE

Cloak the hallowed halls of your home in a veil of drama with black and white decorations that are frighteningly simple to make and find.

UNDER A WATCHFUL EYE
Cut out heirloom relatives into template shapes and assemble them into fractured friends (opposite). Use an urn as a pedestal to command attention. A black bureau (this page) is a befitting stage for a theatrical display, and comes to life with the découpage of a single eye. All directions and templates for paper projects can be found at HolidayWithMatthewMead.com.

NOTHING SAYS HALLOWEEN like a good disguise and a spooky dose of black and white. You can create a spirited, seasonal display in your own home by gathering items of that color palette which you already own and recasting them as creepy props. A good seasonal transformation doesn't have to entail a garish mix of commercial Halloween decorations and embellishments. Here, simplicity reads as elegance, lending a festive vibe that can endure a month-long display without overwhelming the senses. By simply incorporating everyday objects into your décor—albeit by draping them in a shroud of spookiness—you can achieve an element of mystery without showy nods to the holiday. Your rooms will remain familiar and comfortable, with subtle details that guests to your home can discover over time during a party or visit. To achieve this fearless balance, drape tables and mantels in vintage lace or timeworn fabric, layer black and white pillows on sofas and chairs, and forage through your attic or basement for an eclectic mix of vintage collectibles to use in Victorian-inspired vignettes with a thoroughly modern twist. With the addition of some inexpensive store-bought oddities and trinkets and some of Matthew's easy-to-make paper projects, you will be on your way to an ominous Halloween display that will leave family and friends frozen in their tracks, and you worthy of a standing ovation.

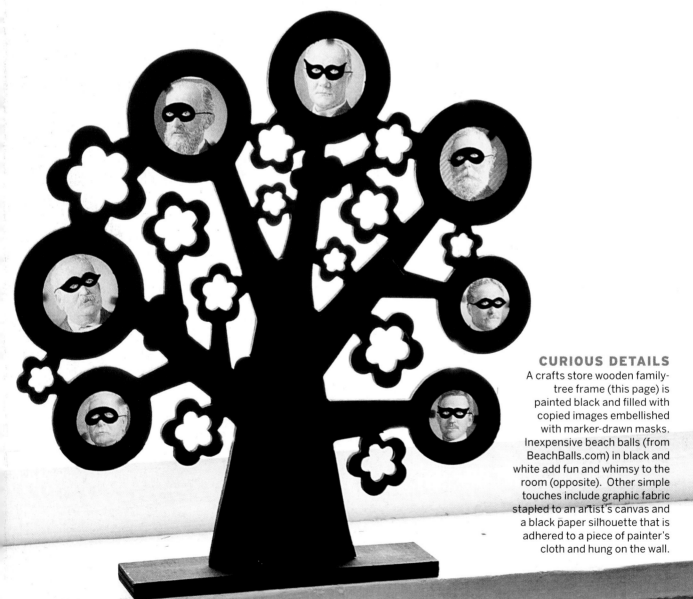

CURIOUS DETAILS
A crafts store wooden family-tree frame (this page) is painted black and filled with copied images embellished with marker-drawn masks. Inexpensive beach balls (from BeachBalls.com) in black and white add fun and whimsy to the room (opposite). Other simple touches include graphic fabric stapled to an artist's canvas and a black paper silhouette that is adhered to a piece of painter's cloth and hung on the wall.

"Hunt for dramatic treasures and curious trinkets that may await you in an old attic trunk." *— Matthew*

ECLECTICALLY YOURS

A framed illustration (opposite), sporting a black mask painted onto its glass, is hung amidst vintage frames. A console table (this page) draped in old crochet mimics a spider's web, while a white glass garden orb symbolizes the moon. A glass vessel, with a copied photo slipped inside, is topped with a witch's hat and sits near a graphic hanging lamp cage-turned-basket.

UNCOMMONLY SIMPLE

Common items can be quick-change artists when grouped together or mixed with easy-to-find craft products. An intricately carved table hosts an elaborate birdcage. Accented with a top hat, it has the subtle illusion of a person, bringing drama to the corner of this small entry. Once Halloween is over, extend the season by simply removing the hat and placing glass jars filled with acorns, pinecones and small Baby Boo pumpkins inside the cage.

GET THE LOOK

1. Vintage mushroom sculptures are transformed with a coat of black paint. Displayed in a grouping, they are a whimsical way to highlight an old silhouette photograph. Scatter a handful of black buttons nearby for a play on a common variety of the popular fungi.

2. A glass cloche brings another family photo from mundane to magical with the addition of a jaunty top hat. Simply photocopy and enlarge your photo to fit under a favorite glass vessel.

3. An old Grecian wall pocket is filled with pearlescent gumballs – a humble offering for tricksters passing by.

4. Print an excerpt from Edgar Allan Poe's famous poem "The Raven" on printer paper and tape to the inside of a lamp to illuminate your décor with subtle melancholy.

5. Marrying two of Halloween's iconic symbols, a vintage black cat's path is crossed by a bold spider.

6. Painted white, a pumpkin is embellished with black paper rickrack and dots to stand out amidst a backdrop of black. Cut out the paper design of your choice and adhere with Zots™ and double-sided tape.

7. Iron-on fusing magically transforms cut felt bats into a startling edging detail for guest room sheets. Use iron-on letters to transform a small pillow into a bedtime greeting.

8. Cast an enchanting spell on a vintage fan using black paper dotted in a graphic paint pattern. Adhere the paper to the fan blades using spray adhesive.

9. Look at cast-off collectibles in a new light. Eclectic finds add style, like this graphic and unique vintage light shade cover. Missing its glass, Matthew turned it on its end and put it to use to corral clusters of candles or vintage scripts. Find blade design and light shade message templates at HolidayWithMatthewMead.com.

1

2

3

4

ever more

5

6

7

midnight

8

9

ELM STREET
SLEEPY HOLLOW
HALLOWEENTOWN
PUMPKIN HILL
DEVIL'S TOWER
TOMBSTONE
SKULL CREEK
DEADMAN CROSSING
GOBLINTOWN
WITCH LAKE
TRANSYLVANIA BEACH
WIZARD'S WALK
SCAREYVILLE
WARLOCK MOUNTAIN
GHOST BOULEVARD
RUE DE DRACULA

DANGER AHEAD
Matthew glued this print to a multi-drawer chest (opposite).
Reminiscent of vintage subway signs, it bears tribute to creepy
destinations. Purchase the print at HolidayWithMatthewMead.com.
A deep and elegant shadow box (this page) elevates a toy spider to
its new status as a rare Victorian prize. A simple sheet of vintage
ephemera serves as a period backdrop to the creepy crawly artwork.

STILL LIFE
A vintage glass display case (opposite) contains faux arachnid friends and their spherical web creations (they sit atop delicate blown ostrich and chicken eggs found at a flea market). A vintage owl statue rests under glass and acts as an eerie sentry in the room. Layered black curtains enclose a bench (this page) punctuated with black and white cushions, painted pumpkins, and a grimacing moon.

NOT SO SPOOKY

There is no need to let the cost of decorating your hallowed halls send chills up your spine. Take some of the fright out of Halloween with some fun and easy projects using what you have on hand.

CANNED GOODS

Look no further than your local candy store or supermarket's produce aisle (even your garden shed!) for easy and inexpensive decorating ideas. Old paint cans — wrapped in photocopied shop ledger's pages and adhered with double-stick tape — are topped with miniature faux pumpkins and a handful of Halloween candies, like these black and white licorice drops and gumballs. Use hot glue to assemble the candy atop the cans and display out of reach of little ones.

CRACKLE...POP
Nothing says spooky like the creaky branches of a dead tree, looming large and black in the dead of night. Create your own tabletop versions using black cardstock. Download the template and directions at www.holidaywithmatthewmead.com. Group several together for a not-so-enchanted forest.
OPPOSITE: Orange poppers, found at a craft or party supplies store, will give guests a jolt as they pull them to reveal the surprises inside. Embellish with black paper and stickers.

"Halloween décor, when simple, should never be boring. Add in a few surprises." — *Matthew*

SWEET AND SPOOKY You know you're going to have leftover candy after the big night: Save yourself the tummy ache and use some of it beforehand to craft some sickly sweet holiday accents. These over-sized candy-studded balls were made using black-painted foam balls from the craft store. Choose candies in Halloween hues and secure using cool glue (Ad Tech™ low-temp glue gun can be found at Michaels) and/or toothpicks, ensuring kids can join in the fun, too. OPPOSITE: Découpage torn strips of black and white scrapbook paper to a dollar store witch's hat and hot-glue vintage buttons around its rim. Display atop a hat stand or glass candle holder.

"Children will nobly help 'disfigure' vegetables

PANTRY PALS Look no further than your pantry or refrigerator's veggie drawer for easy and inexpensive decorating ideas. Arrange peeled carrots in a bowl or apothecary jar, but give them eyes to keep watch for holiday ghouls lurking nearby. Using a paring knife, carve out two small holes in each vegetable and insert a black-eyed pea in each notch. OPPOSITE: Firm, red potatoes are transformed into chubby spiders with the addition of eyes and stick legs. Other common vegetables — including corncobs, eggplant, gourds, or squash — can be doctored, and they look charming gathered together in a wire basket or stacked on a cake stand.

they dislike to make more room for sweets!" —Matthew

BAKE SALE

Halloween is high season for treats. Appeal to everyone's sweet tooth— and their wallets—with a fund-raiser that's perfectly timed.

INCREDIBLE EDIBLES These clever and delicious eats are designed to get your creativity humming with a nice sugar buzz (opposite). Whether you tackle a big project, such as the show-stopping layer cake, or add edible stems to shortbread pumpkin cookies (this page), there are plenty of offerings to keep your baking committee busy. Aren't interested in wielding a pastry bag? Make the signage instead. You can download and print these sharp-looking labels at HolidayWithMatthewMead.com.

whoopie
pies

13c

$1.

cousin
HARRY
cupcakes

SKULLS & CROSSBONES

They may look fierce, but these meringue skulls and crossbones will crumble as soon as they hit your lips. To get the fun shape, line your baking sheet with parchment paper. Draw pencil outlines of the skull and bones shapes, tracing a cookie cutter if desired. Flip the paper so the pencil marks are down, and then fill in the outlines with meringue batter. Use a pastry bag with a wide, flat tip to pipe on the meringue, or spoon on the batter and use a flat angled spatula to smooth it. When the shapes are baked and cooled, add the mouth and eyes using a tube of black icing with a slender tip, which you can purchase from the cake-decorating aisle of the crafts store. See recipes on page 138.

COUSIN HARRY CUPCAKES

Cousin Harry—or should we say Hairy?—cupcakes are sure to be crowd pleasers. Use the pound cake recipe on page 138 to bake cupcakes that are dense and heavy enough to support the top decorations. Frost the cakes with a bit of vanilla frosting, and then place ice cream cones upside down on each cupcake, anchored into the frosting. (Trim an inch off the tip of the cones first, using a serrated knife.) Tint the remaining frosting using a light brown food colorant and fill a pastry bag fitted with a multi-hole tip, such as the #235 tip. Starting at the top, pipe frosting down the cones in overlapping strands to make the hair. To bring Cousin Harry to life, add black frosting sunglasses and a felt derby hat from the doll-making section of the crafts store.

FROSTING TIPS FROM A PRO

Half the fun of these treats lies in their bold, juicy hues. But if you've ever added food coloring to a batter or frosting, you know it's sometimes tricky to achieve bright, tint-perfect color. Professional chef and baker Alison Ladman, who owns The Crust and Crumb Baking Company in Concord, New Hampshire, worked with Matthew to design these treats. Ladman offers her tips for getting the hues just right:

1. Use gels. Sold in squeeze tubes and plastic bottles, gel food colorings are easier to work with in baking. Ladman says the liquid colorants water down your batter or frosting when you're trying to get impactful color. "You'd have to add a bunch of liquid coloring to get these vivid colors," Ladman says, "but it may only take a couple drops of gel." Ladman uses Americolor gels in her bake shop, but she also recommends the gel colors by Wilton (Wilton.com), which are available online and in the cake-decorating aisles of most crafts stores.

2. Start small. As you're mixing your batter or frosting, Ladman says, add just a couple of drops of the color you want to use, such as orange. "If you want a brighter color, add a few more drops," she says. "But it's always best to start with a few drops because you can't take them back if you add too many."

3. Help yourself. Give yourself a hand achieving colors by starting with a similar-tone base. For Cousin Harry's blond hair, Ladman began with vanilla frosting. For the black stripes in the layer cake, she started with chocolate batter. "It will make your life a whole lot easier," she says. "If you start with batter that's too light, you'll add tons more food color to get the color you want."

THE EYES HAVE IT Plump shortbread cookies are irresistible. But when they are the color of green slime and contain an eyeball? Still fetching by Halloween standards. Tint the dough using green gel food color. Form the cookie balls into plump disks and poke your finger into the center to create the dent. Bake the cookies, and while they cool, tuck in candy eyeballs. For the shaggy cake with protruding eyeballs (opposite), mix purple food gel into the cake frosting. To get frosting that looks petable, screw a #235 tip onto your piping bag; start at the base of the cake, add short bursts of frosting, and work your way around and up. "This will be easier if you elevate the cake on a cake pedestal," Ladman says. For the eyeballs, mold colored fondant pieces around Styrofoam balls and poke them into the cake on white lollipop sticks. See recipes on page 138.

1 **2**

3

THE ART OF THE SALE

Every organization has its own bake sale method, but we suggest this novel idea: Ask for a voluntary monetary donation at the door. Then issue guests a standard amount of fake bake-sale bills and coins. The guests use the bills to "pay" for items from various "vendors." (This is especially fun for children to do.) Typically with most voluntary donations, people donate more than what they would have spent on baked goods if they had been using their own money. **1.** A bucket of advertising signs stands waiting to be planted in a stack of whoopie pies or secured next to a candy jar chock full of meringues. Making up odd prices, such as the bewitched number 13, lets kids have fun counting out their money. **2.** Bake-sale bills are handed over for a creamy whoopie pie. **3.** Print off a supply of bills and coins for guests to spend for baked goods. You can send the downloaded files from HolidayWithMatthewMead.com to a color-printing web site, such as FedEx.com/office. Offer guests a supply of wax bags, as well as paper sacks or reusable grocery bags to transport their goodies home. **OPPOSITE:** A black-painted tiered stand offers up a tempting assortment. Scaled down in quantity, this is a tasty array of treats for a Halloween party at home.

whoopie
pies

"These are updated versions of the nostalgic treats we all know and love from our elementary school days. Who wouldn't want to take some home?"
— *Matthew*

MAGICAL TRANSFORMATIONS Orange-tinted shortbread cookies become pumpkins with the addition of marzipan stems. Look for moldable marzipan at specialty food stores, then tint it with green food gels. For the whoopie pies, tint two bright batches of creamy frosting and use a #8B tip to pipe the frosting onto the cookies. Turn red orchard apples into sweet portable treats with candy coatings and twig skewers. To make the skewers, scrub a thin branch with soapy water, rinse, then trim it to 8-inch lengths, cutting at an angle. Find recipe info on page 138.

POOF! THEY'RE GONE! Light-as-air meringues get into the holiday mood with a swirl of black and orange food tint (opposite). To keep the tint from coloring all the batter, paint narrow stripes on the inside of the pastry bag before you fill it with meringue batter. Use a paintbrush dedicated to food, and only paint on a couple of stripes, Ladman says. "When you squeeze the bag and pipe the meringue, it causes the color to twist," she says. The success of this stunning layer cake (this page) lies in vivid color and patient cutting skills. Color vanilla cake batter with orange tint and chocolate cake batter with black tint ("You'll need at least half the bottle to make black," Ladman says.) Bake one orange cake and one black one, and then slice each into three thin layers. Alternate the layers with rich chocolate buttercream icing tinted black. See recipes on page 138.

MAGICAL PUMPKIN PATCH
Gather up the little ones and throw a cheery Halloween party that toasts the bounty of the season and the treats it brings. A tiny mouse (this page) prepares to nibble some cake while a cluster of wooden toadstool cut-outs adorn the party space (opposite). Tiny paper toadstools hang from a branch suspended from the ceiling by clear monofilament line. A light-weight sun statue from the garden is a striking focal point on the table and casts a happy glow.

FOREST FÊTE

For little children, Halloween is best celebrated with a nod to whimsy and happy symbols. What could be sweeter than toadstools?

ON THE SPOT

Think outside of the box to create unique toadstool accessories on a budget:
1. A door stop-sized cement mushroom statue from the garden center becomes a colorful party centerpiece when brightened with acrylic paint. Place it on a metal plate and surround it with gumballs for the party and later bring it out onto the porch as a sweet keepsake. **2.** Intricately patterned paper toadstools hang from a sturdy painted branch that has been suspended above the party table. To make your own, download the pattern at HolidayWithMatthewMead.com and use a paper punch to make holes to slip waxed twine through. **3.** Sweetly humble vintage glasses with an oh-so-fitting toadstool design were plucked from a thrift shop and are the ideal sized tumbler for small hands. Look for them at flea markets and yard sales or try your hand at painting your own using paint that is designed for glass.
OPPOSITE: Paint real or faux pumpkins with polka dots and place around the party room. You will find all toadstool templates on our website: HolidayWithMatthewMead.com.

SWEET TREATS

Every party needs a cake, so bake up our toadstool-themed confection (opposite) using the recipe and directions found at HolidayWithMatthewMead.com. Tint the icing to shades of red and yellow and decorate the top of the cake with melting discs embellished with candy. Fill a bowl with sprinkled sugar cookies (this page) and watch little hands dig in with delight.

1

3

2

EASY DOES IT

Not restricted to just Halloween, a forest theme is the perfect way to celebrate the onset of autumn. Plan simple party activities that children can easily take part in like painting pumpkins and decorating cookies. Each and every element can be created at least a day ahead to leave time for setting the stage for this whimsical party. **THIS PAGE: 1.** Children love fanciful party themes and a bevy of toadstools draws upon their love of "Once upon a time..." **2.** Create an adorable toadstool napkin ring that guests can keep. Download the template at HolidayWithMatthewMead.com and use a Zot™ to adhere it to the napkin ring. **3.** Fill interesting jars and containers like this vintage refrigerator bottle with a fruity punch and ice to quell big thirsts. **OPPOSITE:** Nothing says yummy like peanut butter and chocolate, and kids know it. Keep treats simple by embellishing store-bought peanut butter cups. Decorate each cup with chocolate candy-coated sunflower seeds set into place using piping gel.

Carry on the woodland theme by painting just-picked pumpkins (this page) with three-dimensional circle detailing. Using this photo as a guide, paint the dots in shades of yellow, white, and red and outline some dots in black, using a fine paintbrush. For a healthy treat, fill a stack of enamel bowls (opposite) with strawberries and place candles into several to mark a new celebratory tradition that children will love.

TRICKED OUT TREATS

Not just for nibbling, favorite candies can whet your crafting appetite, too, as ingredients in clever seasonal decorations.

SUGAR HIGHS
Slap a goofy grin on a plain pumpkin using candies swiped from the treat stockpile (opposite). Hot-glue licorice twists for hair curls, gumdrops and sugared fruit gummies for eyes and eyebrows, a shimmery orange gumball for the nose, and wrapped fruity rolls for the mouth. Glasses filled with colored sugars are fitting pedestals for figures made from sugared fruit candies (this page). Stack several shapes on toothpicks or bamboo skewers to form the bodies. Then add features using smaller gummy pieces and colored non-pareils normally used for cookie decorating; use piping gel (a tube of frosting used to decorate cookies and cakes) to adhere the small pieces. For the witch's hair, cut black licorice into strands using an X-ACTO knife.

FLAVORFUL FAVORS

If you have just a few door-knockers on All Hallow's Eve, give away individual treat creations like this handsome skeleton (below). Assemble the body using a lollipop for the head, Tootsie Rolls® for arms, Smarties® for legs, and a box of raisins for the torso, and hot-glue the pieces together. Then wrap and tape each part with black paper, or print the templates from HolidayWithMatthewMead.com. Affix a circle to the lollipop for a face. 1. Twist up a treat-filled cracker, which is a popular party favor in England. Fill empty paper towel or toilet paper rolls with candies, then wrap them in tissue paper and tie the ends with ribbon. Make your own festive labels, or download and print these from HolidayWithMatthewMead.com to tape around the outside. 2. Pick crafting candies based on color and shape, and then purchase them in bulk from candy stores or online vendors. Some sites, such as CandyFavorites.com even let you search candies by color, theme, and holiday. 3. Make irresistible sippers out of colorful glass bottles filled with FunDip®. 4. Fill clear wedding favor tubes from the crafts store with orange and black candies to make fetching handouts. Seal the ends with pieces of scrapbook paper cut and taped in place.

1 2

3 4

"It's so much fun to play with your food, especially when it's candy. I think because it's a goofy medium, you can be more creative. The only drawback is getting sick from eating so many 'supplies.'"
— *Matthew*

FLIGHTS OF FANCIES
Create an exotic scarecrow centerpiece using sugared fruit gummies (this page). The crows are grape-flavored slices, with black-licorice pieces for the beak and wings. For the scarecrow, poke a black-painted bamboo skewer through two orange shapes, then a top hat made from a grape ring and black licorice. Another crow rests atop the hat on another skewer piece. The arms, legs, and belt are black licorice pieces, and the face is brown non-pareils. Put together these puzzles (opposite), and the reward is the candies underneath. Print old-fashioned images from HolidayWithMatthewMead.com, then cut each one into 20 ½-inch squares. Use a roll of tape or a glue dot to adhere the squares to wrapped Starburst® fruit chews.

Kids have always turned licorice twists into mustaches and Chiclets® into teeth. Tap your inner child to look beyond a favorite candy's tantalizing taste to notice its shape and texture, or wrapper color and design as crafting potential.

ABOUT FACE

Candy can be the face, the features, or the head that supports it all. For these standout jack-o-lanterns, we started with plain and black-painted pumpkins, as well as a vintage metal canteen and an old tobacco can painted orange. Then we hot-glued on a variety of candies, including tictacs®, gumballs, licorice laces and pastilles, Sixlets®, and gumdrops to form the expressions. 1. For these skeletons, an Easter egg-shaped candy tin is the skull. The features are cut from black paper and glued on. 2. Perched on a black vase, this tobacco can has Halloween charm. Use hot-glue to adhere licorice-twist hair and licorice-lace eyes. Attach an M&M® candy in the center of the eyes and a taffy for the nose. Gumballs with shiny shells form the mouth. 3. Two coats of matte-black spray paint give this pumpkin a sinister start, but the comical candy smile, fashioned from tictacs®, fruit gummies, and chocolate gold coins for eyes, lightens the mood. 4. Turn foil-wrapped chocolates into handheld jacks by gluing on faces cut from black paper.

1 2

3 4

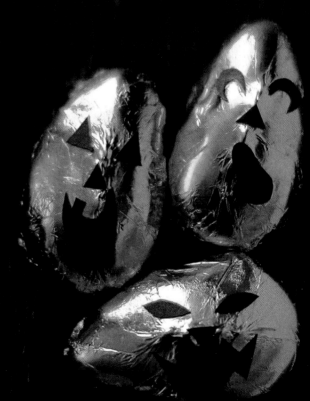

WHITE-MAGIC

Halloween is a holiday normally associated with shades of vibrant orange and deep ebony. The result is often spooky and... expected. Turn tradition on its ear and employ white, with dramatic effect. Indeed, draining the color from your Halloween décor does not mean you will be left with a palette devoid of charm. With a little creativity and decorating magic—using readily available props, white paint, craft supplies, collectibles, and edibles—you can create an enchanting Halloween setting that will bewitch each and every guest.

LIGHT AS PAPER
A hungry caterpillar marches across a rustic table (opposite). Crafted using small paper lanterns, pipe cleaners, and white cardstock—and elevated by an inverted galvanized metal planter—it is a whimsical centerpiece. Fanciful paper party medallions and streamers are hung overhead using clear monofilament line.

1 2

3 4

MAKE IT WHITE Have fun finding and making your own white Halloween décor. **1.** "Potion" bottles, made using favors from Wilton's® wedding collection, are filled with milk and labelled, urging guests to "drink up." **2.** Ice-cream sandwich cookies – made using pizzelles—are rolled in white nonpareils and are a frosty treat sure to chill your guests. **3.** Cream horns become deliciously perfect mummies with the addition of drizzled white icing and candy eyes from the cake decorating department. **4.** Tootsie Pops®, draped in fondant, add up to ghostly party favors that are too cute to spook. Wooden pinwheels (opposite) are sprayed with white paint and placed in personalized party favor bags. White butterflies peek out from small bottles for eclectic table décor. Shop craft stores for similar project supplies.

1

2

3

6

GHOSTLY WHITE

Rummage through your cupboards and head to the craft store to make our ideas. **1.** Chalky paint lends an eerie pallor to an inexpensive rubber bat. Resting on a linen napkin, it is sure to make guests blanch, too. **2.** Candy-coated almonds spill forth from a ceramic owl planter. **3.** A white dinner plate, patterned with a bare branch, has seasonal appeal. **4.** Spicy pfeffernüsse cookies become spooky with the addition of ghostly eyes, created using edible ink markers. **5.** Orange pumpkins, real or faux, can be painted to suit your color scheme. White faux varieties can also be found at most craft supply stores. **6.** Caterpillar directions can be found at HolidayWithMatthewMead.com. **7.** A vintage grate, painted white, mimics the intricate detail of a spider's web.

7

11

12

13

WHITE DELIGHTS

Extend the all-white theme to the menu. White icing, powdered sugar, and vanilla cakes and cookies are common pantry staples. **8.** What is simpler than popcorn served in a milk glass compote? **9.** Scrapbooking page pebbles, which can be purchased in different sizes at craft stores, are a fun way to share a spooky message. Use your computer to print out your own words and place on the adhesive underside of each pebble for a slightly magnified effect. Scatter the pebbles along the table or spell out words of warning at each place setting.
10. A creamy trifle is a white delight and an unexpected Halloween dessert (find the recipe at HolidayWithMatthewMead.com).
11. Frosty vanilla milkshakes are topped with marshmallows and candy eyes.

5

8

9

10

14

BARE BONES

A single color palette can unify a theme, making it possible to incorporate unique objects that can be given common ground with a simple coat of paint. Think beyond just ghosts, witches, and pumpkins. Everyday objects and craft supplies can be used as Halloween décor if embellished or used in an unexpected way: **12.** The owl theme continues with this charming spoon rest, becoming part of the spirited décor. **13.** Wooden flower pot characters from the craft store were sprayed with white paint and given melancholy faces using a marker. **14.** Make personalized treat bags using paper supplies and personalized alphabet stickers from a craft store. **15.** A ceramic owl pitcher serves as a watchful sentry over the festivities.

15

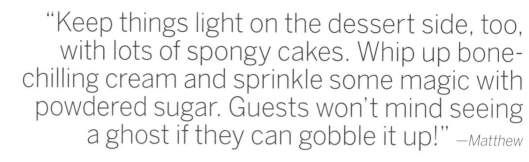

"Keep things light on the dessert side, too, with lots of spongy cakes. Whip up bone-chilling cream and sprinkle some magic with powdered sugar. Guests won't mind seeing a ghost if they can gobble it up!" —*Matthew*

BOO-LICIOUS
Dessert ghosts quiver in fear (this page); they know they won't be around for long! Make them by dusting store-bought sponge cake cups with confectioner's sugar, and then top the cake cups with white chocolate mousse and candy eyes. Set cake stencils atop thick slices of buttery pound cake (opposite) and dust with white confectioner's sugar. Find similar stencils where cake-decorating supplies are sold.

PIRATE'S BOOTY

Chart a course to outdoor fun with a scavenger hunt designed to lead little ones to treats and treasure at the spot marked "X."

SET SAIL FOR ADVENTURE
This ship looks as good bobbing in a pond or docked on a picnic table, depending whether you head to a local park or send the scavengers around your suburban cul-de-sac. Hollow out a sizeable pumpkin, being careful not to pierce the skin if you want to float it. Fill it with chocolate gold coins, and anchor a black-painted dowel with a felt banner into them. Tether the ship to a rock on the bank with a long piece of twine so the kids or their adult escorts can pull it ashore.

GHOST SHIP

"I loved scavenger hunts when I was a child, and this party idea is a way to pass those fond memories along." — *Matthew*

GIVE THEM CLUES

As you plan the route, try to make it age-appropriate. Older kids will want the challenge of hidden markers and obscure references, but young ones don't have the patience once treasure is promised. Make the clues obvious, and don't space them too far apart. Place them at eye level or lower, even if you have to get on your knees to see how they might view the scene. You can find similar ship stencils to paint on a pumpkin path marker (opposite) at craft supply stores.

STAGE THE SCENE

1. The crook of a dead tree is a natural spot for a pumpkin marking the trail. Make sure the adults escorting the wee pirates know the route ahead of time, so no one walks the plank unnecessarily.

2. Brushed onto a thick sugar cookie, this skull design stands out in the twilight hours.

3. A mini pirate ship with a complete set of paper sails waits to be found. Look for balsa-wood boat kits at the crafts store, paint it black, and then add your own sails using bamboo skewers, parchment-color scrapbook papers and pirate-themed stickers.

4. There is a chest of treasure at the end of the route, but everyone will get to take home a bag of goodies, too. Fill clear cellophane bags with gold foil-wrapped candies and white licorice drops. Print off the labels from HolidayWithMatthewMead.com (or design your own) and staple them across the top of the bag.

5. Our little pirate got into the mood by wearing a costume fit for a Captain. Encourage children to wear their Halloween costumes, princess dresses, or pretend-play dress-up clothes. You can also create swashbuckling outfits using foam swords secured with belts of red cloth strips, bandanas for their heads or necks, and fake eye patches from the party goods store.

6. A sprinkling of gold booty in a stream along the path whets the hunters' appetites as they search for the next marker.

PIRATE TREASURE

SCARE 'EM WHITE WITH FRIGHT
Ghostly painted pumpkins are easy to spot in a
decayed tree stump along the trail (this page)
or chaperoning a snack table (opposite). Buy an
assortment of little pumpkins, and adhere eye and
nose shapes cut from self-adhesive contact paper or
shelf liner. Then brush the pumpkins with two coats
of white paint, and when dry, unpeel the shapes.

GO FOR THE GOLD

For the pirate's treasure, Matthew filled an old metal humidor he found at a flea market with foil-wrapped candies, plastic gems, and anything metal that seemed like "booty," such as these ornate brass punch cups. You can look for pirate chests at party goods stores, or try stores that sell imports from India and Egypt for similar engraved metal ones.

THRILL THEM WITH A HUNT

1. Framed up like a snapshot, this black-and-white decal looks like a wanted poster for a pirate ghost. You can download the image at HolidayWithMatthewMead.com. To make an everlasting decoration, adhere it to a faux white pumpkin using découpage medium, such as ModPodge®, and then paint black photo corners to complete the look.

2. Make the treasure map as convincing as possible. Hand-draw it in black ink on a parchment-color piece of paper or a piece of brown paper grocery sack. Crumple the paper and singe the edges with a lighter to create the look of age. After you draw the map, complete with illustrated trail clues, roll it up like a scroll. This can be the party invitation, or just hand it out when the guests arrive.

3. Pirate scavengers fill vintage brass punch cups with colorful gems, costume jewelry, and candies that were purchased at crafts and party goods stores.

4. A brown paper sign, similar to the gift bag labels, marks a handful of treats on the trail. You'll find this and other label designs to download and print at HolidayWithMatthewMead.com.

5. Once you decide where to hide the chest of treasure, mark the spot with a conspicuous X made out of twigs, large pebbles or rocks, or make the mark with sidewalk chalk.

6. A fancy chest brimming with goodies is a tantalizing reward after an afternoon of searching. Reward her efforts by letting her and other guests split the treasure before having autumnal snacks, such as popcorn, pumpkin donuts, and warm apple cider.

ENCHANTED POSSESSIONS

Cast a spell on ordinary household items and everyday collectibles to transform your home for the holiday. Let your imagination run wild with these economical ideas and quick projects.

LOOKS GOOD ON PAPER

Disguise a plant pot as a jolly jack-o-lantern (opposite). This illusion works best on an orange, globe-shape pot, but you could use an inexpensive plastic pot, too. Cut features from black paper and adhere them with double-stick tape. Fill the cavity with candies wrapped in black tulle or stowed inside plastic tubes used for wedding favors. Look for supplies at the crafts store. Turn a secondhand book into a lively 3-D display (this page). Cut a scene from black card stock, then trace around it onto the book pages. Cut the pattern from the pages using an X-ACTO knife, trimming just inside the lines. Fold up the design and glue the card stock to the back with white crafts glue.

1

2

3

FAST AND EASY IDEAS

The best seasonal decorating ideas are the quick ones. No one wants to go to much trouble or time for a 24-hour holiday. These 30-minute projects are short on effort but long on impact. **1.** Transform brown paper craft boxes or leftover jewelry boxes into treat caddies. Brush on thin coats of orange acrylic paint to get a washed look. When dry, draw on jack-o-lantern faces using a fine-tip permanent marker. **2.** A paper parasol becomes an instant costume or plaything. And for kids who hate hot, itchy masks, it's the perfect solution. Cut the design from black paper, and adhere it with hot-glue. If you like this wise owl design, you can download it at HolidayWithMatthewMead.com.
3. Nothing could be more creative than this two-step idea: Paint clean, old shovels with white spray paint formulated for wood and metal. When dry, tape on black paper eyes and prop by the door to tease passersby.
OPPOSITE: An absorbing project for children and adults alike, fill the cubbies of an old tool-chest drawer with seasonal paper cutouts. Don't have a similar drawer? Utensil dividers and office-drawer organizers work, too. Paint the drawer orange, then have fun filling nooks with images cut from patterned scrapbook papers.

"I love being able to find supplies right in my own home to create unique decorations. I'm the only one on my street with ghostly shovels at the door and a plant pot that sprouts a smile." —Matthew

1

2

BEWITCHING CRAFTS

For craft-lovers, here are plenty of ideas to sink your talented teeth into. **1.** Using graphic and boldly patterned scrapbook papers, cut interlocking strips to fashion paper spheres. Fill them with Halloween greetings, funny fortunes, and candies. Download the template from HolidayWithMatthewMead.com.
2. Empty photo frames become a portrait gallery for barely-there ghosts. Remove the cardboard, glass, and backing from the frames. These fretwork frames from the crafts store are black already, but you could paint different salvaged or flea-market frames black. Cut black paper to fit the back of each frame. Cut ghosts from parchment paper. For each frame, place one ghost on the paper backing, then glue the backing to the frame using hot glue. To stick the ghosts to the wall or to have them grip the edge of the frame, use glue dots, called Zots®. **3.** Egg-decorating isn't just for Easter. For everlasting decorations, hollow out raw eggs (look for how-to videos online), and paint them with acrylic paints. You can accomplish the same look by painting plain wood eggs, which you can buy off-season from online retailers. **OPPOSITE:** Paint and display hollowed-out or wood eggs on a vintage printer's rack filled with trinkets of the season.

3

REEL SCARY

Gather fellow movie buffs and plenty of yummy treats and head outside to fire up the projector for a low-budget thriller of a night.

REVENGE OF THE
monster
TOMATOES

MOVIE NIGHT
7PM
snacks and treats

TOP BILLING

Break out the sillies for a night of B-movie viewing in your own backyard. Don goofy glasses and enjoy themed movie snacks while you watch your favorite sci-fi thriller from the Golden Age, when low-budget movies had their glory as the bottom half of a cinematic double feature. Or show one of today's slapstick thrillers that will inspire giggles and some good-natured eye-rolling. Create a movie poster (this page) using Photoshop and place in a painted vintage frame.

SHOWTIME

Create a popcorn station using a vintage floral display stand (this page). Make paper cones from scrapbook paper and fill with popcorn. Here, we accented the stand with faux tomatoes painted with frightful faces. Set up an outdoor movie screen (opposite) by hanging a large white drop cloth or sheet from an arbor or patio beam using nails or hooks. Set out garden chairs, benches, and even exercise balls for plenty of impromptu seating. Hanging paper lanterns and old film reels help set the scene. As soon as dusk falls, bring out a projector and begin the show, letting the good times roll.

THE ICK FACTOR

Creepy concessions amp up the spooky fun: **1.** Buckets of slime add up to hours of gooey thrills (see recipe on page 114). **2.** Navy beans and baby carrots are a fun way to embellish the tomatoes. **3.** Use a vintage movie projector or rent a newer model and invite as many guests as your backyard will host. **4.** A cherry soda with a cherry tomato on top adds up to...smiles! **5.** Googly glasses are a fun prop or take home gift. **6.** Fill a vintage bottle stand with flashlights personalized with stickers. **7.** Children will thrill at the idea of staying up late with friends and treats. **8.** Offer different flavors of popcorn and replenish often. **OPPOSITE:** A test tube stand holds "tomato" cake pops. Create our candy coating faces or use icing to attach paper ones. Find the cake pop recipe, candy face directions, and découpage patterns at HolidayWithMatthewMead.com.

1

2

3

4

5

6

7

8

KILLER TOMATOES

Make a pot of creamy tomato soup (this page) to ward off the evening chill. While little ones may reach for more salty-sweet fare, parents will appreciate the savory soup (see recipe on page 114). Fill small bowls and top bottles of cherry cola with juicy-sweet cherry tomatoes (opposite). Create scary faces by carving out holes for navy bean eyes and teeth and carrot tip noses.

CREEPY CLASSICS
Celebrate the cheese factor of a spooky B-movie by making Gooey Grilled Cheese Sandwiches (this page). For a healthy twist on an old favorite (see recipe page 114) bake in the oven alongside packaged French fries. Place fries in new, parchment paper-lined coffee cups that have been dipped in red paint (opposite), and fill tiny cans of tomato paste with ketchup (use a clean-edge can opener to prevent sharp edges).

BUCKET O' SLIME

Kids will love playing with this slippery concoction

You will need:

- 1 ½ cup water (reserve ½ cup to mix with glue)
- 1 tsp Borax (found in laundry aisle of grocery store)
- ½ cup white school glue
- Red food coloring
- Unused paint cans, available at Home Depot
- Plain, colored scrapbook paper in shades of red
- Tomato Slime label template (found on our website: HolidayWithMatthewMead.com)

1. Pour 1 cup of water into a medium-sized bowl. Add several drops of food coloring to the water. For more vibrant colors, use more drops. Add 1 teaspoon Borax and mix well. Set aside.

2. Pour ½ cup white glue into a separate bowl and stir in ½ cup water.

3. Add the glue mixture to the Borax mixture and mix well.

4. As slime forms, remove from bowl, drain off any excess water, and knead the slime in your hands until mixture feels dry enough to handle.

5. Place slime into an empty paint can and close lid tightly.

6. Using our template, print paint can labels onto red scrapbook paper.

7. Wrap labels around paint cans and secure using double-stick tape.

8. After making or playing with slime, wash hands before eating.

GOOEY GRILLED CHEESE

Fire up the oven to make multiple sandwiches in a healthy way.

You will need:

- 12 slices bread (or more, as required)
- Sliced hard cheese (we used cheddar)
- Spreadable butter

1. Butter one side of each cheese sandwich and place on baking sheet.

2. Butter top of each sandwich and place in preheated oven at 425 degrees for approx. 5-7 minutes on one side; flip sandwich over and bake 2-4 minutes longer, or until bread is golden brown.

3. Let cool slightly on cooling rack; slice each sandwich in half and serve.

4. For a fun variation, create Halloween themed sandwiches using pumpkin-shaped cookie cutters.

MYSTERY CUPCAKES

(Adapted from Joy of Cooking®)

Little ones will be none the wiser that tomatoes are the basis of these tasty treats. (makes 12 cupcakes)

You will need:

- 2 cups sifted flour
- 1 teaspoon baking soda
- 1 ½ teaspoon ground cinnamon
- ½ teaspoon ground nutmeg
- ½ teaspoon salt
- ¼ cup unsalted butter
- 2 eggs
- 1 cup white sugar
- 6 drops of red food coloring
- 1 (10.75 ounce) can condensed tomato soup

CREAM CHEESE FROSTING

You will need:

- 8 ounces cream cheese, chilled
- 6 tablespoons unsalted butter, softened
- 1 ½ teaspoons vanilla extract
- 3 cups confectioner's sugar, sifted

1. Preheat the oven to 350 degrees. Line a twelve-cup muffin pan with paper liners.

2. In a large bowl, whisk together the flour, baking soda, cinnamon, nutmeg, and salt.

3. Using an electric mixer, beat the butter, sugar and eggs on high speed until light and fluffy, about 4 minutes. On low speed, beat in the flour mixture in 3 parts, alternating with the tomato soup in 2 parts, beginning and ending with the flour mixture.

Spoon the batter into lined muffin tins until ¾ full. Bake until a toothpick inserted in the center of each cupcake comes out clean, about 25-28 minutes. Cool the cupcakes in the pan for 30 minutes, then transfer to a cooling rack and let cool completely before icing.

4. To make the frosting, combine the cream cheese, butter, vanilla and sugar in a mixing bowl and mix until just smooth and creamy. If the frosting is too stiff, beat for a few seconds longer, being careful not to overbeat it. Time saver tip: use a tub of prepared cream cheese frosting. Set aside some frosting to tint and use for the tomato detailing on top of each cupcake.

CREAMY TOMATO SOUP

(Makes 6 regular or 12 miniature (½ cup) bowl-sized servings)

Take the chill off an autumn evening with this hearty soup.

You will need:

- 2 tablespoons butter
- 2 tablespoons all-purpose flour
- 4 cups (1 quart) V8® or tomato juice
- Salt and pepper to taste
- 2 cups milk or heavy cream
- Italian flat-leaf parsley
- Cherry and grape tomatoes for garnish

1. In a large pot, sauté onions in butter over medium-low heat until soft and translucent. Remove from heat.

2. Stir in the flour until mixture is smooth and then slowly whisk in the V8/tomato juice.

3. Remove from heat and use an immersion blender to blend until smooth.

4. Return pot to medium heat, season to taste with salt and pepper and bring just to a boil, then immediately reduce heat and simmer 10 minutes.

5. Remove soup from heat and let cool 10 minutes, then slowly stir in milk or cream.

6. Serve immediately and garnish with fresh parsley and halved cherry or grape tomatoes.

KILLER COOKIES

Delightfully dark and ghoulish, these treats offer the chance to slip over to the not-so-sweet side of cookie decorating.

NAME YOUR POISON

Tucked amid potions and antidotes—actually candy-filled apothecary bottles with clever new labels—is some edible poison. Mix up a batch of your favorite cutout cookie dough, and roll it out to ¼-inch thickness. Cut out bottle shapes using a sharp knife, or use cookie cutters designed for us by Victor Trading Co. (VictorTradingCo.com). Coat the baked cookies in brown-tinted royal icing, which dries hard. Then add white fondant "labels" and brown fondant "caps." Finally, draw the label design using edible-ink markers, which are in the cookie-decorating aisle of the crafts store.

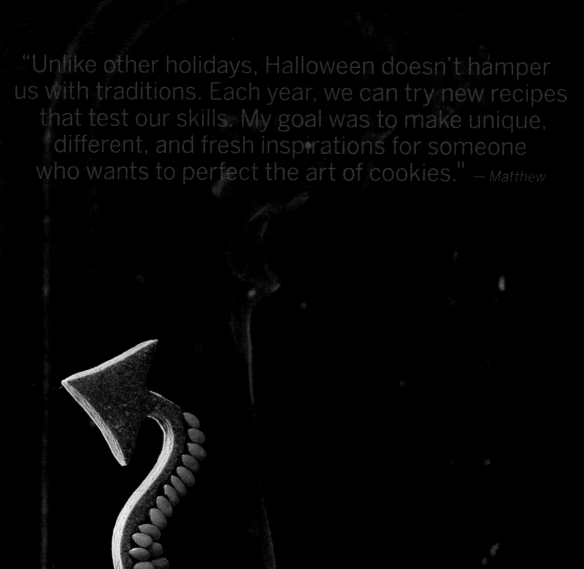

"Unlike other holidays, Halloween doesn't hamper us with traditions. Each year, we can try new recipes that test our skills. My goal was to make unique, different, and fresh inspirations for someone who wants to perfect the art of cookies." — *Matthew*

FROM TIP TO TAIL
Fearsome cookie dragon tails (this page) will thrill at any Halloween gathering. Bake gingerbread cutouts, then use melted chocolate chips to adhere candy-coated sunflower seeds in a scaly pattern along the edge. Beware little critters, the Farmer's Wife has her cleaver (opposite). Mold pliable brown and silver fondant, which you can buy at crafts stores and specialty baking shops, around the baked and cooled cookies. Then dilute brown food coloring with water to create paints that you can brush on to "age" the blade and handle.

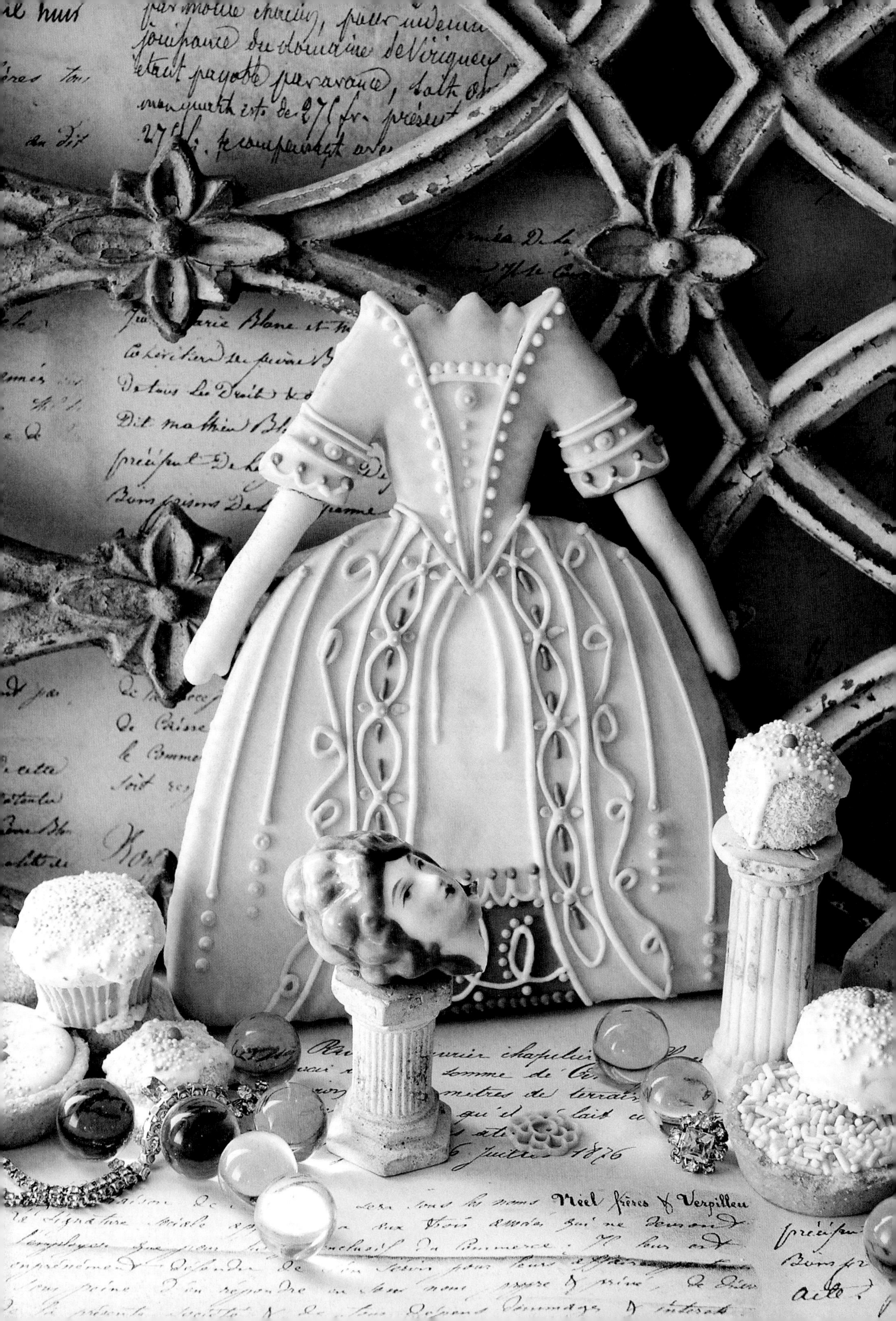
Neel frères & Verpilleu

DISTORTED BODY IMAGES

Off with her head—it's one less thing to decorate after all. Cut out princess or ball-gown-shape cookies (opposite), lop off the heads (or use our headless cutters from VictorTradingCo.com), then bake and cool. Make the elegant gown decorations as fancy or as simple as you like by using tinted royal icing. To create the thin piping, snip off a tiny bit of the very tip of a plastic sandwich baggie, and fill with icing. To get the relief pattern on the cuff of Captain Hook's appendage (this page), use gray-tinted fondant, and sculpt it with a popsicle stick or bamboo skewer. Brush on edible shimmer dust to create the silvery finish.

CULTISH CAMEOS

In profile, these flying witches (this page) seem almost gentle. Use black- and white-tinted royal icing to coat the cookies edge to edge. Then add beads for the hatbands using edible-ink markers. For these loony felines (opposite) the trick is to paint on food coloring to achieve the furry edges. Draw the design using edible-ink markers, then fill in with gel food coloring. You can use regular artists' brushes, but make sure they've never been used.

NOTE: The specially designed cutters used for every cookie on these pages are available from Victor Trading Company (719/689-2346; VictorTradingCo.com).

OVER THE MOON
A paper moon garland hangs over a candy dispensing station created from an old general store rack. Make treat packets by stapling scrapbook paper into sleeves and trim with lengths of scalloped paper. Create numbered star tags by using craft paper and stickers and fill the packets with candy and old photos.

MOONSTRUCK

Experience the many faces of the
moon with these paper crafts
and party treats that will make your
Halloween gathering shine.

"Adults love Halloween, too. With a few grown-up additions, you can host a frighteningly mature fête. Have fun accenting the food and drinks with paper tags and labels we created just for you."

— *Matthew*

WARNING LABELS
Paper tags with foreboding messages (this page) can be downloaded at HolidayWithMatthewMead.com. Two old metal cake stands (opposite) hold jelly jars and pinch bowls filled with M&Ms and mini bread sticks and cookies — offering quick nibbles for guests.

1

2

3

PICK YOUR POISON

At every party, hungry guests gravitate to the food and beverage stations; so a temptingly displayed offering will have guests gnashing their teeth in anticipation. Create a foodie focal point with a multi-level approach to showcasing culinary delights, like the tasty buffet that lines this wooden plant stand (opposite). Attach humorous labels to wine bottles and create party picks by gluing paper tags onto toothpicks to poke into individual servings of ramen noodle salad. Make the salad ahead of time by mixing ramen noodles with sliced scallions and slivered almonds and a few dollops of your favorite salad dressing. Surprise your guests with imaginative serving ideas (this page): **1.** Use a rustic cutting board to serve chicken legs skewered by a creepy scavenger tag. **2.** For additional "glow," line a window sill with bottles of red and white wine that have been affixed with labels that seemingly challenge your guests' palates. **3.** For added spook, create your own napkin rings using craft paper printed with a template featuring a creepy face and detailing, or make your own design by stamping craft paper, trimming to size, and gluing each end together. You can find all tag and label templates and downloads on our website: HolidayWithMatthewMead.com.

BLOODY MARY

CAUTIONARY CONCOCTIONS
Ready to experiment with drinks in a test-
tube? Filled with a store-bought Bloody
Mary mix, these spicy cocktails (this
page) can be sipped with a paper straw
for added nostalgia. Label jelly jar snacks
(opposite) with words of warning.
(Jelly jars: MatthewMeadStyle.com).

1 **2**

3

TAG, YOU'RE IT!

Candy aside, every adult needs a little sustenance to keep the party rolling. As a host, you won't want to toil and trouble over the cuisine so it is perfectly acceptable to oblige guests' offers of potluck-style donations at the door. To keep things organized, draw up a list of easy items they can bring, like dinner rolls, simple casseroles, cookies, or our no-bake pumpkin cream torte (opposite). Made using a store-bought torte shell and filled with a blend of cream cheese, sugar, and canned pumpkin, it is a quick and tasty dessert that will wow guests. Garnish with piped dollops of fresh whipped cream and dust with crushed ginger snaps. Other ready-made items include (this page): **1.** French bread dinner rolls piled into a pewter bowl. **2.** A New Moon pizza – a ready-made pizza crust topped with a face fashioned from olives, sliced mushrooms, and a cheesy nose. (Sprinkle mozzarella cheese onto the dough to mimic the outline of the face, concentrating a more generous amount where the nose should be.) **3.** Create a potluck container cover by layering a sheet of hand-written gift wrap (from BallardDesigns. com) with our clock-face template—adhere using double-stick tape—and secure with twine. Find recipes and paper templates at HolidayWithMatthewMead.com.

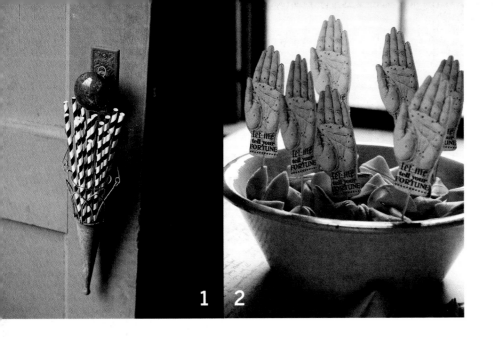

1

2

3

4

5

6

TRICK OR TREAT

Search flea markets for an old comic book stand like this one (opposite) for use as a party favor station. Fill patterned paper bags with adult-friendly goodies like candy, scratch tickets, subway tokens, and vintage jewelry for a fun take on a childhood tradition. Using hot glue, adhere old black buttons to seal each bag and finish with printed name tags.

AN OMINOUS NOTE

When setting the scene at a Halloween bash, keep the ideas creative but the execution simple. Everyday items can be dragged out of the closet and put to a more sinister use with some clever thinking.

1. Gather and place a handful of black and white paper drinking straws into a vintage holder that looks coincidentally like an inverted witch's hat.

2. Fill a large vintage bowl with fortune cookies and insert our "palm reader" party picks. For added fun, replace the fortunes in the cookies with spooky ones you create on your own. You can purchase bulk fortune cookies online or source them via your local Chinese food restaurant.

3. Fill glass jelly jars with single-colored M&Ms and top with a paper moon face.

4. Old jars by the dozen abound at yard sales and flea markets, even in your own pantry. Put them to good use at your Halloween bash by filling them with candy, nuts, or paper strips of ghostly predictions or Halloween jokes to hand out to guests. Wrap the jars in one of our paper labels to take away the mystery of what each jar contains.

5. You can find paper party bags, straws, and more at a variety of craft stores and online stationery and party supplies shops. We purchased our striped straws and dotted bags at Etsy.com/Shop/TheBakersConfections.

6. Highlight a cautionary tale by resting a magnifying glass over two warning labels that can be placed atop an old metal tray, plate or dish. You will find all moon faces, labels and tag templates available to download and print at HolidayWithMatthewMead.com.

HALLOWEEN SCENE

Halloween folk artist and aficionado **Johanna Parker** takes a break from her studio work to chat with Matthew about her whimsical folk art and her take on what is hot this Halloween season. Visit Johanna at JohannaParkerDesign.com and follow the link to her blog and/or visit her at Facebook.com/JohannaParkerDesign.

MM: What do you see as the upcoming trends for Halloween 2012?
JH: As the popularity for the holiday continues to grow, more and more adults are hosting elaborate parties that embrace the happy spirit of Halloween. It's a time to celebrate creativity and craft through fanciful libations, culinary treats, costumes, music, and decor that all scream Halloween. Happily, the passion for collecting Halloween folk art has become contagious and quite chic.

MM: You've expanded your collection of Halloween folk art this year to include carnival-inspired whimsical figures. How do you choose your themes and tie them into Halloween?
JH: Themes are often seasonally driven, so the sights and sounds of the summer carnivals and street fairs leading up to fall have inspired me this year and I also listen carefully to what my collectors suggest.

MM: Do you have a favorite Halloween show you attend?
JH: The Ghoultide Gathering in Chelsea, Michigan is not one to miss. It offers the perfect magical setting for me to exhibit my Halloween folk art along with 30 other very talented artisans. Each contributes his or her unique twist on this haunting genre, and passionate collectors travel in from all across the country to celebrate the art of Halloween and collect from their favorite artists.

MM: Your color palettes are fantastic. What hues have you focused on this year and what inspired them?
JH: Thank you. Currently, I am expanding upon my traditional orange and black motif by adding in magenta, vintage green and turquoise. I love color, and my imagination plays a big role in creating my pattern-filled palette.

MM: Besides collecting your detailed figures, how do your fans display your pieces?
JH: In the fall, I host a blog series that I call Collector Spotlight. Fans of my work, who have amassed a collection, share images of their displays, and it's an opportunity for me to peek inside their homes to see the variety of home environments my work can bridge – from ultra contemporary to country vintage and everything in between! It seems that grouping my figures is a popular way to create a statement, and originals are often mixed in with my Halloween reproductions to create more visual impact.

MM: What is your favorite Halloween memory?
JH: As a young girl, we stopped by my grandparents' house one Halloween night, and my grandmother graciously offered me a pair of her clip-on hoop earrings to complete my gypsy costume. To my surprise, she was permitting me to wear something special that only the big girls enjoyed! I felt so beautiful with them on, and I realized then that Halloween was a special night where rules could be bent and people, big or small, could be whoever they wanted to be without judgement. I still love that.

JOHANNA RECOMMENDS
Visit GhoultideGathering.com, The HalloweenAndVine.com, and EhagEmporium.blogspot.com for information on Halloween artists and events, trends and inspiration, artist links, and online folk art vendors.

COLLECT IT
Visit JohannaParkerDesign.com
to find out where to buy both her
reproduction and original items,
like this adorable clown

BAKE SALE RECIPES

MINI PUMPKIN COOKIES
(makes 12 large cookies)

You will need:

    1 ½ cups butter

    ¾ cup powdered sugar

    3 cups flour

    ½ teaspoon salt

    1 teaspoon pumpkin pie spice

    1 tablespoon vanilla

    8 drops orange food coloring

    ½ cup marzipan (tinted with 4 drops of green food coloring) for stems

1. Preheat oven to 325 degrees.

2. Beat butter with powdered sugar; add in vanilla and orange food coloring.

3. In a separate bowl blend flour, salt, and pumpkin pie spice.

4. Add dry ingredients slowly to the butter mixture and mix until well-blended.

5. Scoop dough by rounded tablespoonfuls and roll into balls. Use the end of the teaspoon to make a divot in the top of each cookie.

6. Bake for approx. 15 minutes. Place cookies on wire rack to cool completely.

7. Make stems of green-tinted marzipan and press into the divot of each cookie.

MERINGUE SKULL AND BONE COOKIES
(makes 1 dozen bones or 6 skulls)

You will need:

    2 egg whites

    ⅛ teaspoon cream of tartar

    ½ cup sugar

1. Preheat oven to 225 degrees.

2. In a small bowl, beat egg whites and cream of tartar on medium speed until soft peaks form.

3. Gradually add sugar, one tablespoon at a time, beating on high until stiff peaks form. Place mixture in a heavy-duty resealable plastic bag; cut a small hole in a corner of bag.

4. On parchment-lined baking sheets with a pencil-sketched template on underside of parchment, pipe meringue into a 3-inch log. Pipe two 1-inch balls on opposite sides of each end of the log. Repeat with remaining meringue.

5. For variation, pipe the outline and fill in the center of a skull design. Smooth meringue with an offset spatula. Bake for 90 minutes or until firm. Decorate skulls with black pre-made icing designs or dust bones with confectionary sugar.

COUSIN HARRY CUPCAKES
Makes 12 regular cupcakes

You will need:

    ¾ cup sugar

    1 vanilla bean

    1 ½ sticks (6 ounces) unsalted butter, softened

    3 large eggs, room temperature

    1 tablespoon pure vanilla extract

    2 cups sifted cake flour

    ½ teaspoon baking powder

    ¼ teaspoon salt

    1/3 cup (3 ounces) sour cream, at room temperature

1. Preheat oven to 350 degrees

2. Place the sugar in the bowl of a stand mixer.

3. Use a paring knife to split the vanilla bean lengthwise, then scrape the seeds into the sugar. Blend on low speed until the seeds are evenly dispersed.

4. Add the butter and beat on medium-high until the mixture is very light—almost white in color; 4 to 5 minutes.

6. In a separate bowl, beat the eggs with the vanilla extract.

7. With the mixer on medium speed, add the eggs to the butter mixture about 1 tablespoon at a time, allowing each addition to completely blend in before adding the next.

8. Sift the cake flour, baking powder, and salt into a medium bowl and whisk together.

9. With the mixer on low speed, alternate between adding the flour mixture and sour cream, ending with the flour mixture.

10. Fill cupcake liners ¾ full. Bake for approx. 20 minutes.

MARTIAN EYE COOKIES
(makes 1 dozen cookies)

You will need:

> 3 cups flour
> ½ cup cornstarch
> ¼ tsp salt
> ½ tsp baking powder
> ½ tsp baking soda
> 1 stick (8 tbsp) butter, at room temperature
> 1 cup sugar
> 1 large egg
> ⅔ cup fat-free milk
> 6 drops green food coloring
> 12 icing eyes from the cake decorating section of the crafts store.

1. Preheat the oven to 325ºF.

2. Cream the butter and sugar together. Mix in the egg.

3. In a separate bowl, combine the flour, cornstarch, salt, baking powder, and baking soda. Pour half of the dry mix into the butter/sugar/egg mixture and combine. Mix in the milk and then add in the remaining half of the dry ingredients.

4. For colored dough, add food coloring and knead the dye into the dough. Wrap dough in plastic wrap and chill for 1 hour.

5. Take the dough out of the fridge. Sandwich one piece of dough between two pieces of plastic wrap on a flat surface. Roll the dough out to 1/8 inch thick and cut with a round cookie cutter.

Place cut-outs on parchment-lined cookie sheets.

6. Bake cookies for 15 minutes; then cover cookie sheet with a piece of aluminum foil to preserve the colors and bake for 10 minutes more.

7. While still warm, place divot in cookie using your thumb. Place icing eye decoration in each.

BEWITCHING LAYER CAKE

You will need:

> 1 package of vanilla cake mix.
> 1 package of chocolate cake mix.
> Black and orange food coloring gel
> Basic Frosting (see accompanying recipe)

1. Grease and flour four 9-inch cake pans.

2. In separate bowls, prepare vanilla and chocolate cake mix according to package directions. Add 6 drops of orange coloring gel to the vanilla cake mix and up to a teaspoon of black coloring gel to the chocolate cake mix. Blend well.

3. Pour vanilla and chocolate batters separately into four cake pans and bake according to the package directions; let cool thoroughly.

4. Using plain dental floss cut three of the cooled cakes in half horizontally to create three layers of each color. (The remaining layer can be set aside for use in making Halloween trifles layered with pudding and cream.)

5. Assemble the six layers atop each other, alternating vanilla and chocolate layers, and spread black tinted frosting between each layer. Finish with a final smooth layer of the tinted Basic Frosting (see recipe below).

BASIC FROSTING FOR CAKES AND COUSIN HARRY CUPCAKES
(yield: 4 to 5 cups)

You will need:

> 4 cups confectioner's sugar
> 1 cup shortening
> 2 tablespoons water
> 1 teaspoon clear artificial vanilla extract

1. In a large bowl, combine sugar, shortening, water, and vanilla.

2. Beat on low speed to combine, then beat on medium speed for five full minutes until smooth and creamy.

**For Bewitching Layer Cake, add 1-2 teaspoons of black food coloring gel for black frosting.

** For Furry Monster Cake, add 6-8 drops of purple food coloring gel for purple frosting.

** For Cousin Harry cupcakes, add 4 drops of warm brown food coloring gel for frosting.

FURRY MONSTER CAKE

This cake is all about the icing! You can create it using whichever boxed mix you like, and prepare and bake according to package directions. We used three nine-inch layers to make this cake, spreading frosting in between each layer, and a #235 tip to create the icing effect. See page 46 for detailed instructions on recreating the icing effect.

HALLOWEEN MERINGUE KISSES
(makes 70 kisses)

You will need:
    2 egg whites
    A pinch of cream of tartar
    ½ cup sugar
    Black and orange food coloring gel

1. Preheat oven to 200F.

2. Line two baking sheets with parchment paper and set aside. In a medium bowl, beat egg whites with cream of tartar until soft peaks form. Beat in sugar about two tablespoons at a time, until stiff glossy peaks form.

3. Fit a pastry bag with a ¼ inch plain tip. Use a small clean paintbrush or cotton swab to brush the inside of the bag with 2 stripes of the food coloring, opposite one another. Spoon meringue into pastry bag.

4. Pipe one-inch cookie kisses, placed one inch apart, onto baking sheets.

5. Bake until cookies are dry, about 90 minutes. Turn off the oven and let cookies remain in the oven another 30 minutes. Transfer to a wire rack and let cool completely. Cookies will keep up to 1 week stored in an air tight container.

BLACK CANDIED APPLES
(makes 8-10 candied apples)

You will need:
    8-10 medium-sized apples
    8-10 wooden twigs, trimmed
    3 cups granulated sugar
    ½ cup light corn syrup
    1 cup of water
    Several drops of cinnamon-flavored oil
    ¼ teaspoon of red food coloring
    ¼ teaspoon of black food coloring

1. Clean and dry the apples and scrub the wooden twigs in a soap and water solution and rinse well.

2. Remove any stems or leaves from the apples and insert a twig into the end of each apple.

2. Heat and stir sugar, corn syrup, and water in a saucepan until sugar has dissolved. Boil until the syrup reaches 300 degrees on a candy thermometer.

3. Remove from heat and stir in flavored oil and food coloring.

4. Dip one apple completely in the syrup and swirl it so that it becomes coated with the melted sugar candy. Hold the apple above the saucepan to drain off excess. Place apple, with the stick facing up, onto a baking sheet that's greased or use a sheet of parchment paper. Repeat the

process with the remaining apples. If your syrup thickens or cools too much, simply reheat briefly before proceeding. Let the apples cool completely before serving.

MAGICAL WHOOPIE PIES
(makes 12 whoopie pies)

You will need:

2 cups all-purpose flour

1 cup sugar

¾ cup milk

½ cup unsweetened cocoa

6 tablespoons butter or margarine, melted

1 teaspoon baking soda

1 teaspoon vanilla extract

¼ teaspoon salt

1 large egg

**Marshmallow Filling Recipe

You will need:

6 tablespoons butter or margarine, slightly softened

1 cup confectioner's sugar

1 jar (7- to 7 ½-ounce) marshmallow cream

1 teaspoon vanilla extract

Purple or orange food coloring

1. Preheat oven to 350 degrees. Grease two large cookie sheets.

2. Prepare whoopee pie batter: In a large bowl, combine all batter ingredients and mix until smooth using an electric beater on medium speed.

3. Drop dough by heaping tablespoons, 2 inches apart, on each prepared cookie sheet. (There will be 12 rounds per sheet.)

4. Bake 12 to 14 minutes, rotating sheets between upper and lower racks halfway through baking, until puffy and toothpick inserted in center comes out clean. With wide spatula, transfer cookies to wire racks to cool completely.

5. Prepare Marshmallow Cream Filling: In large bowl, with mixer at medium speed, beat butter until smooth. Reduce speed to low; gradually beat in confectioner's sugar. Beat in marshmallow cream and vanilla until smooth. Add food color of your choice.

6. To fill cookies, place icing in a pastry bag fitted with a #8B tip. Pipe icing onto inside of the cookie, working from the outside to the middle. Sandwich with a second cookie.

PAINTED PUMPKINS
Truly a quick and easy project, painted pumpkins create a lot of decorative impact without requiring much crafting skill.

You will need:

Smooth-skin pumpkins free of deep grooves and bumps

Sticky stencils or patterns (office labels and kids' stickers work)

Masking tape

Permanent marker

Artists' brushes

Black acrylic paint, such as the DecoArt® brand

Clear acrylic sealer (optional)

1. Working with a room-temperature squash, wipe the pumpkin free of any dust or dirt. Let it dry completely. Moisture from a cold or wet pumpkin prevents the paint from sticking.

2. For a longer-lasting design, coat the pumpkin with a clear sealer and let it dry completely.

3. If you skip the sealing step, draw the pattern directly on the pumpkin skin, using stencils, tape, or stickers to trace the pattern of your choosing. Outline any designs with permanent marker.

4. Fill in the pattern with acrylic paint. Let dry. Enjoy for 1 to 2 weeks.

5. To stack your designs, trim off the stem of the bottom pumpkin close to the skin, then stick a bamboo skewer into it and the bottom of the top pumpkin.

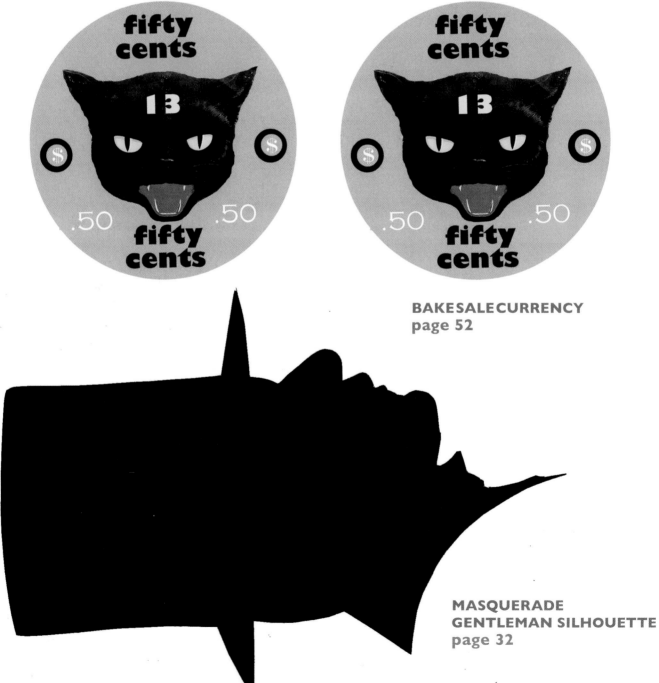

BAKE SALE CURRENCY
page 52

MASQUERADE
GENTLEMAN SILHOUETTE
page 32

MOONSTRUCK TAGS
page 124

leg of crow

PIRATE BOOTY TAGS
page 90

GHOST SHIP

PIRATE TREASURE

X MARKS THE SPOT

NIE NIE'S HALLOWEEN

AS OCTOBER NEARS, my mind shifts to one thing: Halloween. Childhood memories come rushing back as soon as I spy pumpkins on doorsteps and Halloween candy flooding store shelves. As a child, Halloween meant so much more than treats and costumes. On the first Monday in October, my family would gather to eat chocolate donuts from Winchell's donut shop and drink homemade cider. Then, we'd begin our pumpkin carving contest, with the winner receiving $20 to purchase a costume. With eight siblings, I won only once, and happily picked out a store-bought costume – a true luxury in those days. Like most children, my mother directed us to the basement each year to scrounge for bits and bobs to create our own. Weeks before Halloween, my cousin Katie and I would carefully map out our route, and banned dawdling, silliness, or even snacking while trick or treating. We'd return home to gather in front of the fireplace, empty our bags, and begin trading (Tootsie Rolls® were my goal). Now, as a mother, I love helping my children create new Halloween traditions, and still strive to sneak the Tootsie Rolls from their stashes!

"I love vintage Halloween collectibles. They remind me of my childhood." — *Stephanie Nielson*